www.providencebooks.net

Publisher Contact

Email:contact@providencebooks.net

Social media: facebook.com/providencebooks

Acknowledgements

The team at Providence Books would like to thank our friends, family, suppliers and customers for making our vision of creating the highest-quality books a reality. Thanks for purchasing and enjoy the quotes!

This page is intentionally left blank

This page is intentionally left blank

A world free of nuclear weapons will be safer and more prosperous.

Ban Ki-moon

Achieving gender equality requires the engagement of women and men, girls and boys. It is everyone's responsibility.

Ban Ki-moon

All nuclear material in weapons programmes must be subject one day to binding international verification.

Ban Ki-moon

All women and girls have the fundamental right to live free of violence. This right is enshrined in international human rights and humanitarian law. And it lies at the heart of my UNiTE to End Violence against Women campaign.

Ban Ki-moon

Although more than 500 million maritime containers move around the world each year, accounting for 90 per cent of international trade, only 2 per cent are inspected. Strengthening customs and immigration systems is essential.

Ban Ki-moon

Any use of chemical weapons, by anyone, under any circumstances, is a grave violation of the 1925 Protocol and other relevant rules of customary international law.

Ban Ki-moon

Around the world, climate change is an existential threat - but if we harness the opportunities inherent in addressing climate change, we can reap enormous economic benefits.

Ban Ki-moon

As I prepare for my second term as Secretary-General, I am thinking hard about how we can meet the expectations of the millions of people who see the U.N.'s blue flag as a banner of hope. We have to continue our life-saving work in peacekeeping, human rights, development and humanitarian relief.

Ban Ki-moon

As a child growing up during the Korean War, I knew poverty. I studied by candlelight.

Ban Ki-moon

At a time when we aim to accelerate our efforts to achieve the Millennium Development Goals and define a bold agenda for the period beyond 2015, the role of charity can and should grow. U.N. bodies such as the U.N. Volunteers Programme and UNICEF offer venues for people across the world to get involved.

Ban Ki-moon

Border strengthening is effective, but not if done in isolation. We also need to give priority to establishing public institutions that deliver a sustained level of security and justice for citizens. Border security can never come at the expense of migrants' rights. Nor can it be used to legitimize inhumane treatment.

Ban Ki-moon

Building sustainable cities - and a sustainable future - will need open dialogue among all branches of national, regional and local government. And it will need the engagement of all stakeholders - including the private sector and civil society, and especially the poor and marginalized.

Ban Ki-moon

Businesses succeed when societies themselves succeed. When countries are affected by violence and the absence of the rule of law, business can and must be a messenger of peace.

Ban Ki-moon

By including children with different learning abilities in mainstream and specialized schools, we can change attitudes and promote respect. By creating suitable jobs for adults with autism, we integrate them into society.

Ban Ki-moon

By strengthening the three pillars of the United Nations - security, development and human rights - we can build a more peaceful, more prosperous and more just world for our succeeding generations.

Ban Ki-moon

Charity plays an important role in upholding the values and advancing the work of the United Nations.

Ban Ki-moon

Chemical weapons simply have no place in the 21st century. Progress in this vital area will help generate momentum to meet our goal of eliminating all weapons of mass destruction.

Ban Ki-moon

Cities can be the engine of social equity and economic opportunity. They can help us reduce our carbon footprint and protect the global environment. That is why it is so important that we work together to build the capacity of mayors and all those concerned in planning and running sustainable cities.

Ban Ki-moon

Climate change does not respect border; it does not respect who you are - rich and poor, small and big. Therefore, this is what we call 'global challenges,' which require global solidarity.

Ban Ki-moon

Climate change is destroying our path to sustainability. Ours is a world of looming challenges and increasingly limited resources. Sustainable development offers the best chance to adjust our course.

Ban Ki-moon

Climate change, demographics, water, food, energy, global health, women's empowerment - these issues are all intertwined. We cannot look at one strand in isolation. Instead, we must examine how these strands are woven together.

Ban Ki-moon

Climate change, in some regions, has aggravated conflict over scarce land, and could well trigger large-scale migration in the decades ahead. And rising sea levels put at risk the very survival of all small island states. These and other implications for peace and security have implications for the United Nations itself.

Ban Ki-moon

Countries with higher levels of gender equality have higher economic growth. Companies with more women on their boards have higher returns. Peace agreements that include women are more successful. Parliaments with more women take up a wider range of issues - including health, education, anti-discrimination, and child support.

Ban Ki-moon

Defeating racism, tribalism, intolerance and all forms of discrimination will liberate us all, victim and perpetrator alike.

Ban Ki-moon

Do not hide behind utopian logic which says that until we have the perfect security environment, nuclear disarmament cannot proceed. This is old-think. This is the mentality of the Cold War era. We must face the realities of the 21st century. The Conference on Disarmament can be a driving force for building a safer world and a better future.

Ban Ki-moon

Education promotes equality and lifts people out of poverty. It teaches children how to become good citizens. Education is not just for a privileged few, it is for everyone. It is a fundamental human right.

Ban Ki-moon

Equality for women is progress for all.

Ban Ki-moon

Europe and Africa share proximity and history, ideas and ideals, trade and technology. You are tied together by the ebb and flow of people. Migration presents policy challenges - but also represents an opportunity to enhance human development, promote decent work, and strengthen collaboration.

Ban Ki-moon

Every child, woman and man has a right to enough nutritious food for an active and healthy life.

Ban Ki-moon

Every day, we at the United Nations see the human toll of an absence of regulations or lax controls on the arms trade. We see it in the suffering of civilian populations trapped by armed conflict or pervasive crime. We see it in the killing and wounding of civilians - including children, the most vulnerable of all.

Ban Ki-moon

Frankly speaking, I don't know much about rock music. But I enjoyed some when I was in college or high school. But I stopped listening after Elvis Presley!

Ban Ki-moon

Freedom is a timeless value. The United Nations Charter calls for encouraging respect for fundamental freedoms. The Universal Declaration of Human Rights mentions freedom more than twenty times. All countries have committed to protecting individual freedoms on paper - but in practice, too many break their pledge.

Ban Ki-moon

From the beginning of my time as Secretary-General, I have sought to advance a practical, action-oriented vision of the U.N. as the voice of the voiceless and the defender of the defenceless.

Ban Ki-moon

Gender equality and women's empowerment have been a top priority for me from day one as Secretary-General. And I am committed to making sure that the U.N. leads by example.

Ban Ki-moon

Globalization is exposing new fault lines - between urban and rural communities, for example.

Ban Ki-moon

Grave security concerns can arise as a result of demographic trends, chronic poverty, economic inequality, environmental degradation, pandemic diseases, organized crime, repressive governance and other developments no state can control alone. Arms can't address such concerns.

Ban Ki-moon

I am disturbed by how states abuse laws on Internet access. I am concerned that surveillance programmes are becoming too aggressive. I understand that national security and criminal activity may justify some exceptional and narrowly-tailored use of surveillance. But that is all the more reason to safeguard human rights and fundamental freedoms.

Ban Ki-moon

I believe that the topic of chemical weapons is critically important for international peace and security, and I take note of the ongoing debate over what course of action should be taken by the international community. All those actions should be taken within the framework of the U.N. Charter, as a matter of principle.

Ban Ki-moon

I call for greater measures to involve more women at higher levels in mine action. Governments should do more to address gender in their mine action programmes and through their implementation of the Anti-personnel Mine Ban Convention.

Ban Ki-moon

I grew up in war and saw the United Nations help my country to recover and rebuild. That experience was a big part of what led me to pursue a career in public service. As Secretary-General, I am determined to see this organization deliver tangible, meaningful results that advance peace, development and human rights.

Ban Ki-moon

I have been very encouraged by President Obama's call to action on climate change both at his Inauguration and in the State of the Union Address. This is a global imperative. I also welcome President Obama's intention to pursue reductions in nuclear arsenals.

Ban Ki-moon

I have been, and will remain, outspoken in my insistence that Israel has a right to live in peace and security.

Ban Ki-moon

I have run with the Olympic Torch during the 2012 summer games in London and the 2014 winter games in Sochi.

Ban Ki-moon

I look forward to strengthening the U.S.-U.N. partnership and working closely with Secretary of State Kerry towards our shared goals of peace, development, and human rights.

Ban Ki-moon

I take very seriously my responsibility as Secretary-General to make sure that the United Nations is doing everything it can to uphold the universal prohibition on the use of chemical weapons.

Ban Ki-moon

I treasure my meetings with individuals affected by autism - parents, children, teachers and friends. Their strength is inspiring. They deserve all possible opportunities for education, employment and integration.

Ban Ki-moon

I was profoundly moved to be the first United Nations Secretary-General to attend the Peace Memorial Ceremony in Hiroshima. I also visited Nagasaki. Sadly, we know the terrible humanitarian consequences from the use of even one weapon.

As long as such weapons exist, so, too, will the risks of use and proliferation.

Ban Ki-moon

I will do everything in my power to ensure that our United Nations can live up to its name, and be truly united; so that we can live up to the hopes that so many people around the world place in this institution, which is unique in the annals of human history.

Ban Ki-moon

In 2009, at the height of the global economic crisis, it was clear that we were seeing something new: the impacts of the crisis were flowing across borders at unprecedented velocity.

Ban Ki-moon

In the Andes and the Alps, I have seen melting glaciers. At both of the Earth's Poles, I have seen open sea where ice once dominated the horizon.

Ban Ki-moon

It is a sad but undeniable reality that people have died in the line of duty since the earliest days of the United Nations. The first was Ole Bakke, a Norwegian member of the United Nations guard detachment, shot and killed in Palestine in 1948. The toll since then has included colleagues at all levels.

Ban Ki-moon

It is important that the right of Israel to exist should be respected and also the viable Palestinian authorities, in terms of political and financial situation, be supported so that both can live side by side in peace and security. That is a two-state solution.

Ban Ki-moon

Like the United Nations, there is something inspirational about New York as a great melting pot of different cultures and traditions. And if this is the city that never sleeps, the United Nations works tirelessly, around the clock around the world.

Ban Ki-moon

Messengers of Peace such as Midori - and our Goodwill Ambassadors, who work directly with the UN agencies - are dedicated and well-informed and credible advocates on behalf of the United Nations. They help us educate audiences worldwide and rally support on key issues of the United Nations.

Ban Ki-moon

Midori has been a steadfast supporter of the United Nations, as a Messenger of Peace and more recently by encouraging our efforts to achieve the Millennium Development Goals.

Ban Ki-moon

My U.N. five-point plan focuses on preventing proliferation, strengthening the legal regime, and ensuring nuclear safety and security - an effort that was given good momentum by the Nuclear Security Summit held in Seoul earlier this year. The world is over-armed, and peace is underfunded.

Ban Ki-moon

New York is one of the greatest cities in the world. It is a fitting host to its many international visitors, who can come to witness first-hand what a vibrant multicultural democracy looks like.

Ban Ki-moon

Not many countries establish a prize for peace. The Seoul Peace Prize has its roots in the 1988 Summer Olympics when this country opened its doors to people and athletes from more than 160 countries. Korea did so in part because it believes in the power of sports for peace and development.

Ban Ki-moon

Nuclear accidents anywhere can affect people everywhere.

Ban Ki-moon

Nuclear disarmament and non-proliferation are not utopian ideals. They are critical to global peace and security.

Ban Ki-moon

Nuclear disarmament is one of the greatest legacies we can pass on to future generations.

Ban Ki-moon

Nuclear power plants must be prepared to withstand everything from earthquakes to tsunamis, from fires to floods to acts of terrorism.

Ban Ki-moon

Nuclear tests poison the environment - and they also poison the political climate. They breed mistrust, isolation and fear.

Ban Ki-moon

One of my earliest memories is walking up a muddy road into the mountains. It was raining. Behind me, my village was burning. When there was school, it was under a tree. Then the United Nations came. They fed me, my family, my community.

Ban Ki-moon

One of the main lessons I have learned during my five years as Secretary-General is that broad partnerships are the key to solving broad challenges. When governments, the United Nations, businesses, philanthropies and civil society work hand-in-hand, we can achieve great things.

Ban Ki-moon

One of the main lessons I have learned the last five years as Secretary-General is that the United Nations cannot function properly without the support of the business community and civil society. We need to have tripartite support - the governments, the business communities and the civil society.

Ban Ki-moon

Our planet's lands and oceans are already stretched to meet the demands of 7 billion people. The human population continues to grow. The search for sustainable solutions is an economic and a moral imperative if we are to create the future we want.

Ban Ki-moon

Our work for human dignity is often lonely, and almost always an uphill climb. At times, our efforts are misunderstood, and we are mistaken for the enemy. There has been a clear erosion of respect for U.N. blue and our impartiality.

Ban Ki-moon

Our world is one of terrible contradictions. Plenty of food, but one billion people go hungry. Lavish lifestyles for a few, but poverty for too many others. Huge advances in medicine while mothers die every day in childbirth, and children die every day from drinking dirty water. Billions spent on weapons to kill people instead of keeping them safe.

Ban Ki-moon

Pacific Islands are among those that contribute least to global warming, yet suffer most.

Ban Ki-moon

People understand that nuclear weapons cannot be used without indiscriminate effects on civilian populations. Such weapons have no legitimate place in our world. Their elimination is both morally right and a practical necessity in protecting humanity.

Ban Ki-moon

Personally, I do not know whether humankind is alone in this vast universe. But I do know that we should cherish our existence on this precious speck of matter... the greatest gift that could be bestowed upon us. For all practical purposes, there is only one planet Earth.

Ban Ki-moon

Raising ambition in 2014 is crucial for arriving at a meaningful climate agreement in 2015.

Ban Ki-moon

Saving our planet, lifting people out of poverty, advancing economic growth... these are one and the same fight. We must connect the dots between climate change, water scarcity, energy shortages, global health, food security and women's empowerment. Solutions to one problem must be solutions for all.

Ban Ki-moon

Schools connect children to their communities. Jobs connect adults to their societies. Persons with autism deserve to walk the same path.

Ban Ki-moon

Since I became Secretary-General, five years ago, I have seen youth participate at the United Nations as never before.

Ban Ki-moon

Some might complain that nuclear disarmament is little more than a dream. But that ignores the very tangible benefits disarmament would bring for all humankind. Its success would strengthen international peace and security. It would free up vast and much-needed resources for social and economic development. It would advance the rule of law.

Ban Ki-moon

Strangely, charity sometimes gets dismissed, as if it is ineffective, inappropriate or even somehow demeaning to the recipient. 'This isn't charity,' some donors take pains to claim, 'This is an investment.' Let us recognize charity for what it is at heart: a noble enterprise aimed at bettering the human condition.

Ban Ki-moon

Sustainable development is the pathway to the future we want for all. It offers a framework to generate economic growth, achieve social justice, exercise environmental stewardship and strengthen governance.

Ban Ki-moon

Terrorism is a significant threat to peace and security, prosperity and people.

Ban Ki-moon

The Arab Awakening or Arab Spring has transformed the geopolitical landscape.

Ban Ki-moon

The Czech Republic is a dynamic United Nations Member State, active on the Human Rights Council, contributing to the peaceful settlement of disputes, and helping other countries to achieve a democratic transition.

Ban Ki-moon

The Fukushima Daiichi nuclear disaster in March 2011 was an immense tragedy that sparked a global response. The international community came forward with aid to the victims and came together to address the broader concerns about nuclear security and safety.

Ban Ki-moon

The Millennium Development Goals were a pledge to uphold the principles of human dignity, equality and equity, and free the world from extreme poverty. The MDGs, with eight goals and a set of measurable time-bound targets, established a blueprint for tackling the most pressing development challenges of our time.

Ban Ki-moon

The U.N. might not be the most luxurious place to work, but it certainly is one of the most important places in the world.

Ban Ki-moon

The U.N.'s humanitarian agencies rely on charitable donations from the public as well as the generosity of governments to continue their lifesaving work in response to natural disasters, armed conflicts and other emergencies.

Ban Ki-moon

The U.N.'s impartiality allows it to negotiate and operate in some of the toughest places in the world. And time and again, studies have shown that U.N. peacekeeping is far more effective and done with far less money than what any government can do on its own.

Ban Ki-moon

The United Nations has a proud record of helping millions of people in mine-affected countries.

Ban Ki-moon

The United Nations is committed to ridding the world of anti-personnel landmines.

Ban Ki-moon

The burden for achieving disarmament cannot be borne by peace groups alone. Everybody, regardless of age, income, profession, gender or nationality, has a stake in this quest.

Ban Ki-moon

The catastrophic humanitarian consequences of any use of nuclear weapons require that it be treated as a top priority. Disarmament will work better than any alternative in reducing the risk of use.

Ban Ki-moon

The clear and present danger of climate change means we cannot burn our way to prosperity. We already rely too heavily on fossil fuels. We need to find a new, sustainable path to the future we want. We need a clean industrial revolution.

Ban Ki-moon

The explosion in access to mobile phones and digital services means that people everywhere are contributing vast amounts of information to the global knowledge warehouse. Moreover, they are doing so for free, just by communicating, buying and selling goods and going about their daily lives.

Ban Ki-moon

The good name of the United Nations is one of its most valuable assets - but also one of its most vulnerable. The Charter calls on staff to uphold the highest levels of efficiency, competence and integrity, and I will seek to ensure to build a solid reputation for living up to that standard.

Ban Ki-moon

The human family is at a critical juncture. The world is moving through a great transition. This transition is economic, as the digital revolution advances and as new powers and groups emerge.

Ban Ki-moon

The possibility that terrorist groups could obtain weapons of mass destruction should not be dismissed as a fiction. This is a horrific threat the international community should take seriously. As long as these weapons exist, so, too, does the risk of their use - by accident or design.

Ban Ki-moon

The tragic nuclear accident at Fukushima underscored the urgent need to enhance nuclear safety and the international emergency response framework. I commend the International Atomic Energy Agency for its work.

Ban Ki-moon

The true measure of success for the U.N. is not how much we promise, but how much we deliver for those who need us most.

Ban Ki-moon

This Earth is our only home. Together, we must protect and cherish it.

Ban Ki-moon

Throughout human history, in any great endeavour requiring the common effort of many nations and men and women everywhere, we have learned - it is only through seriousness of purpose and persistence that we ultimately carry the day. We might liken it to riding a bicycle. You stay upright and move forward so long as you keep up the momentum.

Ban Ki-moon

To measure the success of our societies, we should examine how well those with different abilities, including persons with autism, are integrated as full and valued members.

Ban Ki-moon

True security is based on people's welfare - on a thriving economy, on strong public health and education programmes, and on fundamental respect for our common humanity. Development, peace, disarmament, reconciliation and justice are not separate from security; they help to underpin it.

Ban Ki-moon

We are using resources as if we had two planets, not one. There can be no 'plan B' because there is no 'planet B.'

Ban Ki-moon

We have a legal and moral obligation to rid our world of nuclear tests and nuclear weapons. When we put an end to nuclear tests, we get closer to eliminating all nuclear weapons. A world free of nuclear weapons will be safer and more prosperous.

Ban Ki-moon

We have a legal and moral obligation to rid our world of nuclear tests and nuclear weapons.

Ban Ki-moon

We have international standards regulating everything from t-shirts to toys to tomatoes. There are international regulations for furniture. That means there are common standards for the global trade in armchairs but not the global trade in arms.

Ban Ki-moon

We have reached a new milestone as a human family. With seven billion of us now inhabiting our planet, it is time to ask some fundamental questions. How can we provide a dignified life for ourselves and future generations while preserving and protecting the global commons - the atmosphere, the oceans and the ecosystems that support us?

Ban Ki-moon

We must confront persecution faced by many Christian communities and the intolerance that plagues us. We must overcome anti-Semitism and the prejudice that divides us. We must defeat Islamophobia and the fears that weaken us.

Ban Ki-moon

We must eliminate all nuclear weapons in order to eliminate the grave risk they pose to our world. This will require persistent efforts by all countries and peoples. A nuclear war would affect everyone, and all have a stake in preventing this nightmare.

Ban Ki-moon

We need to bring sustainable energy to every corner of the globe with technologies like solar energy mini-grids, solar powered lights, and wind turbines.

Ban Ki-moon

We need to tackle energy poverty.

Ban Ki-moon

Weapons of mass destruction violate more than individual lives - they cross international borders and jeopardize all people. They also drain resources that could be used instead for medicines, schools and other life-saving supplies. We must come together with even greater determination to prevent a WMD nightmare.

Ban Ki-moon

When I was six, the Korean War broke out, and all the classrooms were destroyed by war. We studied under the trees or in whatever buildings were left.

Ban Ki-moon

When Nelson Mandela walked free, the world sang with joy. Ever since, South Africa has stood as a beacon of hope for Africa.

Ban Ki-moon

When food prices surge, poor families suddenly find themselves unable to afford enough nutritious food. If this happens during the first thousand days of a child's life, the damage to his or her body and mind can be permanent.

Ban Ki-moon

When we put an end to nuclear tests, we get closer to eliminating all nuclear weapons.

Ban Ki-moon

Whether addressing immediate crises or building long-term foundations of peace, the United Nations will remain committed to solutions that advance the global good.

Ban Ki-moon

Within the U.N. itself, I have appointed a record number of women to high-level positions. I did not fill jobs with women just for the sake of it - I looked for the best possible candidate, and I found that if you strip away discrimination, the best possible candidate is often a woman.

Ban Ki-moon

Women and girls are disproportionately affected by landmines. They have different needs when it comes to education about risks. And they may face greater challenges when a family member is killed or injured.

Ban Ki-moon

Women can drive progress towards the central goals of mine action, which aims to increase security, rebuild communities, reclaim land and end the looming fear caused by explosive remnants of war.

Ban Ki-moon

Women hold up more than half the sky and represent much of the world's unrealized potential. They are the educators. They raise the children. They hold families together and increasingly drive economies. They are natural leaders. We need their full engagement... in government, business and civil society.

Ban Ki-moon

This page is intentionally left blank

This page is intentionally left blank

This page is intentionally left blank

This page is intentionally left blank

This page is intentionally left blank

www.ingramcontent.com/pod-product-compliance
Lightning Source LLC
Chambersburg PA
CBHW071152280526
45787CB00003B/1492